SOCIAL MARKET

BEGINNERS 2023

Learn how to grow your social media

with beginner's strategy updated for

this specific year; this book provides

you easy and organized knowledge

ready for you

TOM RUELL

Copyright © Tom Ruell 2023,

All rights reserved

Table of Contents

Introduction 4

Chapter 1: Startup 11

Chapter 2: Instagram Marketing Strategy 56

Chapter 3: Tiktok 79

Chapter 4: The Ultimate Marketing Strategy 91

Chapter 5: The LinkedIn Market 114

Chapter 6: Pinterest as media platform 148

Conclusion 173

Introduction

Let us quickly go back in time, say 2002, and suppose you want to make a document public or a book and also set up a blog; you are probably sure that you'd be successful, but you are only worried about one thing, you do not know how to make sure that this book of yours reaches the intended recipient audience, or who could enjoy this book. However, just a few types of advertising were available during that time, such as print ads, billboards, radio, direct mail, direct sales, and television. All of these methods were prohibitively expensive, whose efficacy could not be determined, and which did not allow you to advertise your content to a proper audience, implying that your book would never reach the audience it deserved. Now let us look into and pay attention to this very same scenario in the present day, alongside traditional forms of advertising. You would have entree to digital marketing as a method of marketing that's a lot more profitable and price-reasonable and configurable marketing that would aid marketers to advertise to their listeners digitally using mediums like search engines, websites, social media platforms, emails, to mention a few. Among these types, social media marketing seems like the most eye-catching. Social media marketing would give you as a product deliverer the prospect to take advantage of social media platforms to publicize your content to a highly targeted audience. It would also help more people learn about your book and increase the interaction with your audience. And the best part is that it is relatively inexpensive unless you go into advertising. This whole social media platform will also help you get marketplace insights that might help in understanding your audience preferences better. Let us further assume that you started by taking up a certification process to learn about social media marketing. Since you are already familiar with the whole concept of social media marketing, your next step will be to learn about the different types of content you could display on social media. Some of the most public forms of content you could post would be images, text, posts, polls, and videos. Still, over time you will probably begin to notice that not many people are being exposed to your content anymore.

You start to realize that you need to advertise your content for specific channels, that you would have to employ the advertising alternatives offered by social media networks such as Facebook, Instagram, YouTube, Linked-in, and Twitter as most of these advertising platforms offer users several different options such as image ads. These ads comprise solo or numerous descriptions that are nice-looking and have the optimum quantity of writing. They also include a rallying cry that stimulates user participation. You can now use images from your book to advertise on websites that sell your book and more. Currently, there are texts and post ads. These ads could promote posts or excerpts from your blog or your book, further garnering interest from an exciting audience.

You might also employ video advertisements that include favourable reviews and customer testimonials to advertise to your readers, and you could also use lead ads through which you could collect information from users involved in a weekly newsletter or regular updates from your blog. But the truth is that these are not the only things you could do with social media channels; you could create a brand for yourself and drive audience interest, engage with them, create an identity, engage with content, and find content that works for them you. Social media platforms will also allow you to develop audiences based on demographics such as their age, location, gender, and much more, and over time you will see an increase in the number of visitors coming to your social media page, and therefore your blog. You will also see an increase in the total number of individuals who bought your book, significantly increasing your audience. This book has some of the most crucial things to learn about social media marketing, a step-by-step approach for getting your goods out there and getting massive returns and pulling in relevant attention, and a moderate upturn in profit and presence creation of your brand and product.

Some of the things addressed in this book include;

How to set quantitative, intelligent goals and follow a constant deadline.

How to understand your audience by engaging and connecting with them.

How to set up a social media calendar to plan competitions polls, surveys, videos, and more.

How to use tools for lead generation creating email lists, setting buyer personas, and more.

How to perform visual storytelling with the help of images and videos.

Now the question that might be bothering you could be that how would I be able to lay my hands on all of these?

Before we begin to shed more light on these questions, let's ask ourselves these questions. What can you do with social media marketing? How does engaging with your audience play a vital role in marketing? What is the relevance of your method of determining your target market based on demographics?

All these questions will answer your questions when we begin to answer them.

Chapter One

Startup

You would agree with me if I said the world that we live in now is a highly digital place, but the reality is; that wasn't always the case until four years ago, so if we rewind, letting people know about your products was a little more complicated then. So even if you go back, say five or ten years in time, promoting your products wasn't as easy as it is today. People had to resort to good old-fashioned newspapers, putting an ad on those big thick books called the Yellow Pages that usually sat in your closet and weighed a ton. These and more were ways through which people had to get their product and service out there even though it seems so archaic looking at it now, but back then, that was legitimate, that was the way to do it, and then suddenly, one thing made our lives a lot easier. It came and disrupted the space of marketing. Now let us begin to answer some of these questions keeping us at the edge of our chairs since we picked up this book. I will tag this part as "Introduction to the edge." You know how you can have the edge over a whole lot of other people just because you have a piece of information that they do not have or you are aware of something that they have no idea. We will begin to pay attention to this part of the story here.

How to have "the edge" over others

How can you get started with social media marketing so you can stand out from the crowd by utilizing this fantastic platform that we all use today? First, let us define the core notion, which is what social media marketing is in and of itself: social media marketing.

"Social media marketing involves increasing website traffic it centres engagement it offers you the ability to increase your brand awareness, and it has other marketing goals so you can create various forms of content for different social media platforms."

So that's really in a nutshell what social media marketing in itself is. That is basic, generally known information. The quest is usually to increase our traffic or engagement like the likes or comments; you need to understand marketing principles on social media platforms. Engaging with our users, customers, and potential and prospective clients can put a personalized experience using social media marketing. If the idea is to create different forms of content like videos and blogs, and infographics, and other types of graphics with the potential, actually to go "viral", and what we would mean "viral" is spreading like wildfire, one user sending it to another as rapidly as can be and before you know it, you get millions of views and millions of likes. That right, there is social media's influence on marketing. The following question would be the "WHY", why we need to do social media marketing? Let's dig a little deeper. We mentioned in our definition of marketing on social media that are we have the opportunity to build our brand awareness, and that is no more truthful than with social media marketing, more than any other digital marketing channel. We can improve our brand by pushing out appropriate content to reasonable people using social media marketing. It allows us to put our brand in a good light, in a good position in the vicinity of the right eyeballs, allowing us to improve our brand by pushing out appropriate content in front of reasonable people. For this the social media is a beautiful platform. We can also look at conversion rates to see if we're presenting the right product or service in front of the right individuals.

We build a funnel of prospective customers who turn loyal customers into lifetime customers. We could see it at every step in the process, that our conversion rates may increase, we can undoubtedly leverage social media marketing for SEO (Search Engine Optimization) for search engine rankings, which is basically about posting content on social media platforms to build up the most efficient traffic. We need to understand that you will accede to some benefits from an efficiently working SEO and social media side-by-side; it is very cost-effective if these are efficiently and strategically combined. Now, if you're posting content on Twitter or Facebook, it doesn't cost you anything; it just might require a small amount of time and creativity. Now, if you decide to go ahead and do some advertising on these platforms, yes, it is going to cost you, but you would be surprised that it is not going to be as costly as other search platforms like Google or Bing, where you are paying for keywords and also per click for those keywords. So, social media marketing can be very cost effective and also increase top funnel traffic, so here we begin to see that it goes all the way back to brand experience and brand awareness, as you're putting yourself in position to get noticed by your target audience. When your target customer sees your brand for the first time and learns more about it, they progress to buying a product or service from your brand and then returning to buy another product and service. They then continue to buy that product or service. This is without argument increasing the top funnel traffic, and this is not just the traffic, but the conversions also. This in the long run means that at every step in the process social media allows you to build that funnel depending on where somebody is, whether they're seeing your brand for the first time or actually returning to purchase the product, or service again. And this is the inherent benefit of these platforms, these unlimited possibilities with product consumers and clients. These are the intrinsic benefits of social media marketing.

As we talk about social media marketing, we will most definitely need to discuss using the potential channels used for social media marketing. Social media marketing is already a channel in itself, so let's look at the platform you can use to establish social media marketing efficiently. Now, there are some prevalent platforms, so if you can't tell just by these logos, you probably have not used social media marketing or social media platforms before or taken part in social media.

The Social Media Language

These are the most popular platforms, but hundreds of social media platforms exist.

When we talk about social media marketing and competing, we will start to see anything from microblogging to video-sharing like YouTube, networking platforms like LinkedIn or bookmarking sites, or content sharing sites like Reddit, Q&A, sites like Quora.

Now let us start to address some of the most popular social media platforms, and that's Facebook.

Facebook has an average of (2.27 billion) two-point two seven billion monthly active users. That number is fluctuating since we talk about billions of monthly active users. Up to 88% of all users are on mobile, so what does that tell you? That means Facebook has an app and that app is viral; people tend to use the app more than they use the webpage for Facebook, as they do not necessarily need to log on via the internet on their laptops, or PC. They go right to the app, it's just easier to disseminate information, more accessible to add, friends, comment, respond and so on. It's no surprise that 88% of all users use mobile now (66%) Sixty-six percent of monthly mobile users use Facebook daily, so a lot of recurring users are going back on a day-to-day basis. And what Facebook offers is the opportunity to get information from the people you trust, care about and like to work with. You could also share a group with people you have a common interest with. You could also partake in the same organization, maybe have the same scheme, having the same group with the same passion. I think that's what Facebook is, the commonality it establishes among people. And if you build up a network of that commonality, it is going to be addicting to take part in them. It is also part of what makes Facebook addictive because it bridges the gap between distance and sometimes the feeling of knowing that you are part of somebody's life daily by just being on Facebook.

From an end user's perspective, thinking about it further makes sense. If you are thinking about digital marketing, you will see that two-thirds of a group of individuals or multiple users regularly use it, and there are billions of active users there.

Facebook is evenly matched or say distributed between males and females. If you are targeting the older generation, or if you are targeting the younger generation, or if you are targeting half as female and half as male, then you know that somewhere in there, your target audience is probably on Facebook. Also, your demographic is likely going to be on Facebook.

Facebook now allows for video content to be posted all day long, so if you have YouTube videos, you can share those videos on Facebook. Videos, just like on most platforms, tend to provide better engagement in capitalized industries.

Some of the most liked pages on Facebook span many brands, but let's take a look at Coca-Cola, for example.

Coca-Cola says that Facebook is great for everything. The brand is not necessarily trying to promote only their product, they are trying to use Facebook to build up brand awareness. A huge fortune company like Coca-Cola is not just using Facebook to push e-commerce or a product. This is an excellent example if you can relate the leverage in this simple concept. Knowing how you can leverage on what you want to portray of your brand per time and what Facebook has to offer. And that would also include brand awareness, community building, sharing your content, and updating information not only about the company, as you can see in this case of Coca-Cola, which is situated in Atlanta, Georgia in the United States. You can see what they do here. I think this is a good example, and of course, it is a great example, because the Coca-Cola company is big and known worldwide.

Still, the great thing about Facebook is that you can always take a peek at what other companies are doing. Whether you have a million-plus people liking your page, or a hundred plus people like in your page. You can always get ideas how they are leveraging Facebook. Owning a brand or company would mean there is demand for publicity on you; there is a demand to reach out to more people. You can create a Facebook page for your business just like Coca-Cola, which means you want to separate your business from your carrier. Like everything you do, whether you are writing a blog or creating a video, you want to have original content relevant to your audience. You want to use Facebook for some promotion, but every post does not necessarily need to be marketing your item or service. Looking at how the Coca-Cola page is strategized, it is not always only about the product; it is also about what they are doing for the community. This indicates that they are doing more community-based posts, which to me is original content, positive content, and content that isn't necessarily pushing their product. You could probably argue that: - "Hey it's Coca-Cola, they have the biggest brand in the world." But think about your product and services, think about your brand. If your brand stands for something, like a global level impact, the ecosystem, or the environment, you probably want to be pushing outposts in that direction.

People who are like-minded on Facebook are going to like your page, engage with your content, and tell others about it, so you want them to know what you represent as a brand. You always want to go regional, you always want to be true to yourself and accurate to your brand. Then you could take advantage of user-generated content like sharing a user's experience of using your product. In other terms, it would mean that, if somebody is engaging with you or they have posted something about your brand and product, you can reciprocate, you can undoubtedly post something similar to what somebody's doing with your product or brand. That is an excellent way to create some original content by taking advantage of what the users have generated. Many more prominent brands have a larger space and community reviews.

Now, if you are selling t-shirts, then you can put something in there to help you sell that t-shirt. The Coca-Cola's strategy is: - "Hey! What can we do to help build up our community? What can we do to fundraise?". You can use this strategy as well, too.

Facebook has many features, such as posting polls, including an Instagram feed, adding testimonials and getting creative. You should also be honest with yourself. Before you know it, you're going to start building up a community, gaining a reasonable amount of several likes on your business page, as well as some other tips. Now, for Facebook, when it comes to content you want to schedule your content, you don't want to just continue to post back-to-back. You want to space your content out. Another great advantage to Facebook is advertising, as I already mentioned about social media marketing. Facebook owns Instagram, and they have a great tool for communicating called Facebook Messenger.

You can advertise using Facebook messages, and you can leverage Instagram. What you need to do is go to Facebook's ad manager and create a campaign. When you go to create a campaign, you will be able to click on placements, depending on what you are trying to do, let's say you're trying to build brand awareness. You can do this by using Facebook, Instagram, or a number of other things.

Within Facebook you have different ads available to you from single image ads to video ads, to carousel. When it comes to advertising on Facebook, you have a lot of options, but the biggest one is your audience.

So remember, Facebook has old, young and everyone in between men and women, and so you. Can specifically target interest. You can specifically target gender and age allocation. Using Facebook allows you to focus on who your audience is, and that's the great thing about Facebook. They have a lot of users, so you have an opportunity to reach a specific group of people.

Facebook also has metrics that you can look at to really understand how people are interacting with your ads, how people are interacting with your post. If we go to Facebook, you can click on insights and you can see some insights on posts that I've been posted on your page. You can get insights into how many people viewed it, how many people liked it, how many people engaged, how many people you reached with your post. You can have information about videos followers. Facebook provides recommendations, which is part of Facebook Insights. It will give you feedback as to how your post is performing on Facebook, and you can view metrics related to how your ads are performing. You can see how many people clicked on an ad, how many people reached the ad, how much you've spent. You can look at it by demographic. You can even see cost per results. So you can get a lot of good insights into how your ads are performing as well. If you're running a Facebook campaign targeting a specific audience, you can look at the stats and metrics surrounding the campaign. If you have any questions, you can take a look at the videos on the simplilearn's YouTube channel, and for your Facebook page.

Let's look at Instagram, which is owned by Facebook.

Instagram is a place where you can actually promote your brand, product or service through the power of imagery or video. The average number of monthly users on Instagram is 1 billion, and 32% of all internet users are on Instagram. It's very easy to use, you just need your phone and you can upload an image. That's what makes Instagram so popular. Because it's just a simple tool to use. 60% of all Instagram users are women, so it tends to be more female than Facebook. 59% of the audience is younger than 18 to 29. If these particular demographic and age groups tend to fit your target audience, then

Instagram is a place you probably want to use for social media marketing. The magic content that works best is our photos or videos. I would always prefer videos if you have them available, but photos are always the good way to go. Photos always tell a thousand words, a thousand stories, and a thousand interpretations. Even if you don't have the videos, you can still use images to show your brand in a good light.

It is open to most industries, but the ones that tend to be most successful are beauty, food and fashion. As you can imagine, there are between 18 and 29 year old women on Instagram.

No food beverage always works well when you have video and imagery. Likewise, beauty. But if you're selling that t-shirt or shoe, Instagram allows the platform to work in a way where people can purchase that product. So that's why it tends to work well with e-commerce. There are lots of channels just like on Facebook. If you have a product or service you'd like to promote, then Instagram is the way to go just for brand awareness. If you're selling shoes, then why not take images of them? It's very simple to use. You simply need some hashtags to go along with that photo of a shoe or photo of a cup of coffee, and Instagram will take care of itself. If you have photos, they do accentuate the product, so you should use it to build up brand awareness for a particular product.

Some best practices on Instagram are to have a compelling bio, a good profile picture, and a link to a landing page. You can also leverage emojis. If you have to set yourself up nicely on Instagram, you know if you're in a particular industry like food and beverage, you should follow other food and beverage brands like Coca-Cola, like Starbucks. Just make sure they are relevant and get hashtags. You know, when you post a photo, you should throw some hashtags in there and you can see what other people are hashtagging on Instagram. You can ride the wave of what's trending or create your own unique hashtag. Use both photos and videos. Videos tend to work well on pretty much any platform, and they tend to work well on websites and blogs. You can also get shoutouts from other influencers on Instagram, especially in beauty, especially in food and beverage fashion. Another industry that has a lot of influencers, so please feel free to reach out to them. Reciprocate to see how you can work together where they can actually give you a shoutout on your product. If you want to keep your Instagram account updated, you can update those with Instagram stories. An Instagram story is a short video that shows off a product in a few seconds or even a minute. They're very popular and easy to use. You could even run contests to boost engagement, for example, if your particular product is a particular food like a hamburger, you could post a contest about it, allowing your followers to post the best good-looking tasty hamburger as an example. Or it could be something else in terms of engagement.

There are things you can do to spur engagement on a platform like Instagram where people like to post photos, so what is your best outfit on a Friday night? I mentioned this earlier with Facebook ads, you can run Instagram ads to give a particular post a boost. If we take a little snapshot of what we have available, you can choose from a variety of options in the Facebook

Ads Manager, and probably also select Instagram as the particular platform. If you want to advertise an Instagram when you go to your placements, you could choose either the feed or the stories. You could choose one of these two options. If you want to get more people to see your posts, you can buy some extra clicks. It depends on what you're trying to post, who else is posting, and the cost per click tends to slant a little bit lower. Instagram feed and stories could be a good option if you want to get people to notice a particular product.

Now, let us focus on the business-to-business platform called LinkedIn.

LinkedIn is a very powerful popular business-to-business platform. It has 260 million active users monthly, and unlike Instagram, where it focuses more on women, LinkedIn focuses more on men. 57% of the users are men, but still, you have a lot of women involved in on LinkedIn, so a nice mix between both genders. 38% of the user base are Millennials. There are a lot of young people and older people from different business segments, different levels of business, different business industries, and different verticals. Don't be shy about LinkedIn if your demographic or target audience tends to be older. Just because 38% of the users are Millennials doesn't mean anything. It just means that everyone's using it. If you're in the business of generating business leads, then LinkedIn is the place for you to go.

There are opportunities for you to advertise on the platform. You can also post lots of different types of content on LinkedIn, such as blogs, news articles, tips, and best practices.

You always want to create an engaging profile. There are a lot of opportunities here when I say first things first, make sure it's done.

You also want to be able to post a lot of information about yourself, about what you're affiliated with, what jobs you've held, what groups you're associated with, what your interests are, what certifications you have. You want to be able to complete your total profile. You can create a company page for your business. On LinkedIn, you can just search for simplilearn and take a look at their business page.

You can see here that simplilearn is posting some of the accolades others have, but they're going one step further. Also, they should be posting information about upcoming events and webinars, so they should be posting a mix of different content. That's ideal for any social media platform.

Just like you can on Facebook, just like you can on Instagram, you can boost a post per post so you can get that post in front of some additional eyeballs. You want to improve your companies web page for searches, so it comes down to how many people are following you. When you optimize your company page, just make sure it's complete with some compelling content, and then increase the number of followers you have. The great thing about LinkedIn is that you can simply look at other people's profiles.

If I go back to the home page, you can see who's following what, and LinkedIn does give you opportunities to connect with people. If I go to you, you will be able to see other people that have viewed your particular page and you can connect with them, pay or connect with people who are like-minded or similar, or connected to you. LinkedIn does a good job of showing you other people you can connect with, so it makes it easier for you to get more followers. Having an engaging company page means that both your personal and the company page have all the content necessary, and then increasing followers by posting unique content. The key to LinkedIn is that you can use different media, such as videos and slideshow presentation images, to boost content. You can boost content on LinkedIn if you want to get that content in front of eyeballs.

So let's take a look at an example of a campaign and what you could do on LinkedIn in terms of sponsored content.

If you go to LinkedIn's campaign manager, you can choose to put your ad in front of a specific audience. It depends on who you're trying to target. Facebook is more personal, while LinkedIn is more business-oriented. You have an opportunity to target a particular industry, a particular company, a particular job title, so you can go ahead and create an ad. The ads have imagery to support the ad. Basically when you set up your ad you set up your target. The placement you choose is going to be able to see who you are actually targeting, and you can go ahead and create something about it. LinkedIn has different ad formats, and you can get really creative with who you want to target. Just like Facebook, LinkedIn has some metrics that you can measure and figure out how your particular campaign performed by impressions buy click.

So, the difference between Facebook and LinkedIn is that you can choose the type of people you want to connect with on LinkedIn, while Facebook is for everyone in terms of advertising.

.Let;s talk about YouTube. YouTube currently has 1.9 billion active users, which would make it the world's second-most used search engine. All big markets like to use YouTube, but it's popular across the world just like Facebook where the app is popular. The highest number of monthly active users starts at the United States, Brazil, Russia, Japan and India. With YouTube being a video platform, you definitely need videos because the app is very popular and 70% of all views are generated from mobile. There are a lot of industries on YouTube, and most successful brands.

Combining video and text is a great way to get people to engage. When creating videos on

YouTube, you want to optimize your video for SEO to get views. At the very least, you want to make sure you use the right keywords, title, and hashtags. To optimize your videos, you want to upload regularly and set a schedule for your videos, because if you start to get followers on YouTube or subscribers, they're going to expect you to make more videos. We're not saying you have to make a video once a day. Start out small and build up to a regular schedule, and then you can make a playlist with your videos. At simplilearn, you can see how their videos are broken down into playlists by going to their YouTube channel and seeing it. YouTube also has the ability to provide translations, since it is global. If your target audience is from another country, it probably wouldn't be a bad idea.

Like Facebook and Instagram, or LinkedIn, you can advertise on YouTube. You would just need to do that through Google Ads. With Google Ads, you're going to say, "I want to advertise on YouTube," and you have plenty of options available to you. Anything from pre-roll to appearing in the middle of a video, to appearing before, or at the conclusion of a video. You have a lot of options for advertising on YouTube, and just like Instagram, there are a lot of influencers.

You are welcome to reach out to these influencers on YouTube and see if you can collaborate in some way. For example, you could post their video on your channel, or you could post your video on their channel.

Let's talk about Twitter now. Twitter is a micro blogging platform, so when I say micro blogging, I mean you can only post a limited number of characters, but it's very popular.

It has 326 million active users per month and tends to slant towards Millennials. A lot of young people use it and a lot of people use it to get their news. No longer are the days of going to a newspaper or going to a media news site online. You can quickly go to Twitter and get all your news right there in a feed.

Let's take a peek at Twitter. Here, you can find everything from someone posting something specific about their dog to a particular job, to industry news, to basically an advertisement, to a specific news article. You can find it all here on Twitter in your feed, which is why Twitter does offer videos. Yes, videos are effective. If you go back here, you can see a video of Antonio Brown. A video of his news conference and another promotional video are posted. As you can guess, there are industries that capitalize on Twitter. So, that doesn't necessarily mean that you can't use Twitter for your brand. It really comes down to your target audience. Some of the most influential brands are more focused on news and media. Cosmetics, gaming companies, and everyone is on Twitter.

Ultimately, it comes down to whether or not this platform has your target audience and given the nature of the platform. On Twitter, you can get your brand's product or service out there in a lot of characters. Some other advantages and best practices you can use on Twitter is Twitter cards. All Twitter cards allow you to attach rich photographs or videos to tweets, as well as different media experiences. Rich media, such as videos and images, can be attached to tweets, which can help drive traffic and engagement to your website. Users who tweet links to your content will see a quote-unquote card appear in the tweet, which is visible to their followers. So, that's how it works. I would certainly look to get Twitter cards implemented if you are going to use Twitter as your platform of choice for social media marketing, because it allows you as an advertiser, or as somebody leveraging social media to really enhance your tweet. It provides a better experience for the end user who is looking at your tweet, similar to LinkedIn, where you can really take a look at who's trending and what's trending on Twitter. You can find a list of who to follow on Twitter, which is similar to what you have been posting or similar to your industry. You can then look at trends, you can look at what hashtags are trending, and if you click on a particular hashtag, you can follow a particular person or organization who tweeted something. So that you are always reminded who to follow on Twitter, it makes it easier for you to pick and choose who to follow and build up your following fairly.quickly. Because Twitter actually provides you with opportunities to follow people, just like LinkedIn, just like YouTube, just like Instagram.

There are influencers out there who have a large number of followers and who tweet original content on a regular basis. These are influencers and these are the people you want to engage with.

Look for people on Twitter who are influential and follow them. The rule of thumb is that if you follow someone on Twitter, they're likely to follow you back. So if you can engage with them and follow influencers, you have the opportunity to see not only what they're tweeting, but the ability to communicate with them and engage with them. Maybe they'll retweet one of your tweets and get that tweet out in front of their followers. And the unique thing about advertising on Twitter is - you can promote your tweet just like you promote a post on Facebook or Instagram or LinkedIn but more than any other social media platform, Twitter is the use of hashtags. So, don't be afraid to use appropriate, relevant hashtags. I always use a unique hashtag, but it depends on what I'm tweeting about and if there's something that's trending. Twitter will indicate what is trending in terms of hashtags. If it's something you're tweeting about, then go ahead and use the hashtags as well. A tweet can have multiple hashtags, so don't be afraid to use the unique hashtag with a trending hashtag. The whole idea is to get your tweet noticed.

You can use Twitter chat or other tools that are available to allow you to find people to follow and these people may be interested in your product or service because you believe they will appeal to your target market. For that reason, you can network with like-minded people in the same business or who sell similar goods or interests. Tweet shots are available for that reason.

You want to take advantage of these tools because it's easy to build a following with Twitter, but you want to build a following that will engage with your tweets.

When we talk about all the social media platforms, we talk about Facebook, Instagram, LinkedIn, Twitter, and YouTube - all those are most popular platforms. But at the beginning, I said that there are hundreds of social media platforms out there, and if you're posting content on a number of them, you want to be able to organize it and schedule it. Where it makes sense and when it makes sense, you want to stay organized. There are tools available to help you stay organized, like HootSuite, Buffer or Sprout. Certain tools are available for free trial or low monthly costs, so regardless of whether you're using a free version of one of these tools or another tool listed, or whether you're actually paying for it, it's worth the investment. If you want to do social media marketing, it's worth it to have a social media tool available to help you schedule.

Social media tools help you schedule, but they also do a lot of other things, for example they help you measure the engagement of your posts. I would like to give an example of one of them like Sprout social, so if I go to sprout social here, I can see how my post gets engaged. I could see engagements on certain platforms. I can schedule my post as well. I can pick a time and date to schedule them. And so, I can go ahead and post something and put it in a queue to be published, for example, tomorrow or next week. These tools can help you a lot, like they help you find new followers, give you detailed reports, and help you stay organized, so I think it's worth the investment to look at one of the tools mentioned here.

These are some of the more popular ones. You might even find a free version, but it's still worth the investment to make sure you're scheduling your post at the right time. It's nice to be able to go into a tool like Sprout social and go to reports and measure how Twitter is performing or how Facebook is performing, or how LinkedIn is performing. Many of these tools provide nice reporting options and scheduling options, so you can find more content you can create using them..

Again, you can schedule efficiently analyze them and you can use insights to improve your campaign. This is why these tools give you nice insights into how the post was actually engaged. You want to be able to leverage that. Some of these tools have social listening, which is watching what's being posted online, so you can see what else is being posted and if it's interesting or relevant, you can go ahead and follow it.

Many platforms have social listening as a feature so let's take a look at some tips to be a good social media marketer. Some of the important things you should take care of are to set up a social media marketing plan.

When you set up a social media marketing plan, you need to decide what platforms you want to use and what your goals are for each platform. Before you choose a platform, you should figure out what your objective is in terms of social media, so your objective could be different on each platform. It could be brand awareness on Facebook or promoting a particular product on Twitter. Your objective is going to be on each platform. You want to be able to choose your KPIs and align your KPIs with each platform.

You need to determine what metrics are relevant to your business goals and what kind of material you'll post on different social media networks, so you need to get organized and put a plan in place. Then you want to create informative, shareable material. What I mean is that you want to create unique content. That doesn't mean you can't leverage what other people are doing. If I'm in the shoe business, I can certainly go to Nike or adidas or Puma, or Reebok and see what kind of posts they're putting out. And I could take their cue and do something similar, but I want it to be unique to me and I want it to be unique to my brand. I also want to be able to keep my content visually appealing. I want to be able to use as many photos and videos as I can because videos get better engagement. I want to be active and responsive with my customer base, which means that the whole point of social media is to engage people. People are going to respond, comment, and take part in what you post. Whatever they do, you want to be able to respond accordingly, whether that is positive or negative. And then you want to measure metrics like conversion rates and click the rate. That goes back to putting a plan in place. Figure out what your metrics are. And then, after you've posted on a particular platform, you want to be able to use the metrics to make sure you're achieving your goals. So you want to have those metrics in place beforehand, and then you want to be able to use those metrics moving forward to make sure you're posting what's working and what's not working.

Chapter Two

The Insta-Marketing Strategy: Instagram Marketing Strategy

Instagram, a quirky and engaging image-sharing software, has taken the world by storm since October 2010. Hundreds of millions of Instagram users use filters and frames to turn ordinary photos and videos into memories shared with the rest of the world. Instagram is almost likely a good place to look for photographs and videos of your business. This material serves as genuine peer-to-peer recommendations of your company, which is effectively free promotion. You can only assist in compounding this impact by implementing a strong plan of your own, building brand loyalty, and generating sales as a consequence. Many people have even referred to Instagram as "The World's Most Powerful Selling Tool," such as the amount of enthusiasm shown by its members. These individuals are under the age of thirty, are engaged, and many of them are consumers.

Understand the "Culture of Instagram" and how it works.

The top-performing companies on Instagram all have one thing in common: they understand what distinguishes the app from additional social networking sites and how to take advantage of this understanding to increase their reach and sales. The notion of "Instagram culture" will undoubtedly evolve, but at its heart, users are proud of the material they create and share with the world - you won't find hundreds of impetuous selfies and hazy nightclub shots from the most successful "artists," for example. As a result, designers place significant priority on quality rather than quantity. With creators devoting significant time to meticulously compose and construct photos and videos, cropping and editing until they are perfect, so that when an item is finally posted to their Instagram feed, it is gushed over by delighted followers, complemented by a flurry of likes and comments, and attracts new followers in the process. One of Instagram's most popular slogans is "discover beauty everywhere," encouraging users to look for beauty everywhere they go. To achieve this, companies must demonstrate their worldview through imagery that goes beyond the common perception of them, as well as provide a glimpse into the lifestyle that your product or service makes possible, both through your own eyes and those of customers who use your products or services. Overall, while visual imagery for social media platforms like Facebook and Twitter may occasionally be more ad-hoc in nature, and Pinterest may be more simple and mood board-y or sales, your preference on Instagram should be more creative, arty, and special. It would help if you placed even more emphasis on visual storytelling, turning ordinary situations into artistic moments, and capturing the essence of your brand throughout. Make it a point to become immersed in the culture of Instagram by including more imaginative photos or videos in your feed (which clearly expresses a defined personality and voice as well as mirroring the attitude or preferences of the majority audience), and you'll be in a significantly powerful position from the start.

What are the qualities of a high-quality Instagram photograph, and how do you create one? As you are now aware, just putting any old picture into Instagram will not cut it with the app's sophisticated audience; you must be much more creative and discriminating in your posting. Talking about discovering what kind of photographs Instagram wants firms to publish to keep customers happy, one of the greatest places to start is by looking at its suggestions for Instagram ads: There is no excessive use of picture filters as a means of masking the "truth" of a photo, and no use of text overlays is permitted. Brands are not permitted to use their logo in Instagram advertisements unless it is a natural and unobtrusive setting element. Images used in advertisements must be "authentic to your brand," which means they must not be surprising or corny, and they must not use gimmicks. Photos for advertisements should depict "moments" rather than things. In other words, advertisements must be more than simply a photograph of your goods; they must be something unique and exciting. Ads should use ideas and signals from the current Instagram community, particularly popular hashtags, to be effective. Continue to keep these principles at heart as you go through the remainder of the chapter's guidance and consider how you want to structure your own Instagram strategy.

In the same way that a lot of social media theory doesn't apply to every circumstance all of the time, these principles might serve as a good foundation for your activity. It's very fantastic stuff. By the way, there's a ton more material and strategy for Instagram advertisements available on the internet.

Instagram Profile Optimization is important. Create a profile picture suitable for a circle in your Instagram bio and optimize your bio.

One of the simplest and most efficient ways to communicate with potential followers is to optimize your Instagram bio. Give folks a cause to follow you by describing what sets you apart, remind them that they'll be among the first to know about special offers and promotions, first to get a sneak peek at new product lines, and first to enter Instagram competitions; use the complete 150-character limit for a chance to win great prizes. Do not forget to include the URL to your website in your bio area as well — this is the only location on Instagram where a link will be clickable and visible to others. Maintain a light and amusing tone while using relevant keywords (SEO), an Emoji if the mood strikes you, and a business-specific hashtag, among other things. In an interesting twist, many businesses are deliberately choosing to comprise a link to their blog rather than a link to their online store, demonstrating how they view Instagram as an opportunity to gradually build their brand image as a whole rather than "force" people into making a purchase right away. If you are the company's face, it is also critical to add a photo or profile of yourself (preferably with a cheerful look) or your corporate logo since this will serve as your company's official representation throughout the service. For the same reason as Google+, Instagram (at least on its mobile version) prefers a circular profile picture, which complements people's faces more than corporate logos.

Post only your finest photographs, and get inspiration from other people's work. The most significant companies on Instagram are incredibly selective about the images they put on their accounts. Quality, rather than quantity, is paramount for your portfolio on Instagram. It is essential that you take your time in assembling a collection of images that you are pleased with and that represents your finest work since it is this that will attract readers' attention both when seen as individual pieces of content and when browsing through your gallery as a whole. Many of the most well-known firms on Instagram only post once or twice a day, sometimes even less often. Here are a few basic photography concepts and recommendations to help you enhance the overall value of your Instagram work: Photos on Instagram have traditionally been squares – similar to an old Polaroid photograph – This is still the most common layout technique on Instagram nowadays. Before the shutter of your widescreen camera view is closed, attempt to visualize how your design would seem like a square once the sides have been cropped. When it comes to Instagram photos, the 'rule of thirds' is firmly embedded in many of the best ones. However, when there is a key aspect of your material that a court will annoyingly clip out, the same goes for other kinds of photography. Imagine that your viewfinder has been divided into thirds, horizontally and vertically (or that you have turned on the iPhone Camera grid view through the Options menu); now, balance your composition between these three sections. Obtain symmetrical photos that appear fantastic on Instagram and other social media platforms. You'll be left with a perfectly square crop of your picture at the end of the process. When taking a snapshot, the essential thing to keep in mind is is to keep yourself centered and ensure that all of your lines are completely straight. Make use of angles and lines to your advantage. Instagram is about enabling its users to see the world in new ways. Everyone is used to seeing the world from head height, so try shooting from high and low perspectives, as well as from behind and to the side, to add interest and excitement to your photographs.

Additionally, consider including lines into your photographs - whether they are natural components such as a line of trees or a road that stretches into the distance - to pull people's attention into the picture or towards whatever it is that you want them to see. Do practice concentrating on specific aspects of items or services to attract clients, rather than blander long or mid-range photos to make the most of the comparatively little real estate available on mobile devices (where most of your Instagram material will be seen). The quality dye and material in a garment may be highlighted in a clothes store's advertisement, while a decorating business would choose something more abstract and utilize the close-up view of paint and brush to indicate a job well done. Look for sources of inspiration. If you're having trouble staying inspired, check out Instagram's Explore page (the compass points symbol) to observe the newest developing trends on the platform and try incorporating them into your work practices.

Consistent filters and image editing helps to distinguish your photographs. Instagram's popularity has soared in part due to the simplicity with which users can change regular images into something extraordinary with the app's vintage filters. While these overlays continue to be a key part of the app's appeal, the app's image editing tools have evolved in response to competition to include a variety of additional options for photo tweaking, such as straightening, lux, brightness, contrast, tilt-shift, sharpening, and other effects. With a simple slider, Instagram enables you to control the intensity of each of the adjustments. Overall, I'd recommend subtly applying them (to align with Instagram's preferred approach for brands, which is natural) and selecting a filter that you will use consistently; one that helps the image to reflect your brand culture and personality (e.g., fun, playful, serious, professional), and one that makes your style instantly recognizable within the feed of your fans. Filters may play an essential part in developing a unique branded Instagram account, learning what your followers enjoy about you, and creating consistent material with that theme.

Consider capturing your images on a different platform besides Instagram. If you take a picture inside Instagram, you are immediately obligated to use the app's filters and editing tools to modify it. Despite how many these choices have gotten, it is frequently preferable to take a shot using the built-in camera software on your smartphone (or any other digital camera). If you follow these steps, you will have a 'clean' picture that can be loaded into any photo editing product you like after that (VSCO Cam or Afterlight, for instance - tools that may provide a more unique and diverse filter and image editing options). After that, you may import the picture into Instagram for final editing before uploading it when you're through with it; this is how the experts can create such stunning photographs, which are incomparably different from anything that can be produced alone on Instagram. Of course, if Instagram currently gives you the appearance and feel that you like for your images, that is also acceptable!

Instagram Marketing and Content Plan

Make the most of the picture caption that appears alongside every image on Instagram - It's a small but essential part of your marketing plan. - and never leave it blank. Instagram Marketing and Content Strategy; Make use of it to anchor the substance of the image and convey your company's personality and tone of voice. Examples of utilizing the picture caption include a description of the product you're promoting, asking a question, or initiating a debate, including a call to action and a URL you want your followers to see. Because URLs published inside Instagram descriptions cannot be clicked on, make sure they are short and memorable and use a site like bit.ly to help you with this if needed. Referencing the previous point, another common approach to drive clickthroughs from Instagram captions to your chosen location is adding a sentence such as "click the link in our bio" in the caption. Because your bio is constantly accessible with a single touch, and because the "Website" URL there is currently live, it will save folks the time and effort of opening up a new browser and manually putting in a URL, if that is their choice.

Unlike other social media platforms, Instagram captions do not have a character restriction. For certain businesses, such as National Geographic, this technique results in captions that read like mini-magazine articles. Combining it with high-quality photographs allows viewers to get more engrossed in their material for a longer period, allowing them to experience them as more than just snapshots. Do you need to update a caption to fix an error or add more detail? Select "Edit" from the drop-down menu that appears next to your picture.

Don't be spammy with your hashtagging; instead, follow the latest trends. When you include #hashtags in your Instagram captions, the material will be paired alongside other photographs with the same hashtag and made into clickable links to the photosets containing the content. Because hashtags can be used to find content on Instagram, making use of the appropriate hashtags might assist you in getting your content in front of individuals who are looking for keywords and phrases linked with your company (words in your description that are not preceded with a hashtag will not be taken into account when a user searches). Assuring that your hashtags accurately describe your content will make it easier for visitors to locate you. General hashtags such as #clothing or #food may bring in a few new followers, but they're also quite popular, and your material may get lost in the shuffle when people search for them. Using more precise and descriptive hashtags will give you a far higher chance of getting discovered and followed. For a different approach, whole Instagram communities may be developed around a single actionable, custom-created hashtag - and this is a strategy that works across all social media platforms. Create a hashtag connected to your brand and use it to bring consumers together. Please encourage them to use the hashtag and reward them with likes and comments when they do. Study the most popular hashtags within your company area and include them in your approach. It would help if you also tried using popular but not overused hashtag trends on Instagram to help define your content. Among the most popular of these are #thingsorganizedneatly (a topdown photo of several related items, such as a full outfit or multi-piece toolset, organized in a manner that is pleasing to the eye; often compounded by the use of complementary colors), #fromwhereistand (a first-person, top-down photo of a person's feet, with an emphasis on footwear and the ground below to tell a story), #onthetable (elegant top-down photos of (marking the end of the week with an eyecatching symmetrical scene from your store, city, or elsewhere). While browsing Instagram, you will note how over-the-top hashtag use can be, especially considering that each picture or video may only include a maximum of 30 hashtags. Although this generous limit helps people - who are frequently anxious for an audience - garner a few different views, I would not advocate using such an obvious strategy for commercial purposes since it might come off as spammy, dilute your marketing message, and harm your brand's reputation. Trackman, a competition analysis business, discovered that utilizing between 4 and 5 hashtags boosted Instagram engagements but that using more than five hashtags decreased engagement on the platform. More than three hashtags in each post, similar to what is done on Twitter, in my opinion, will make the content appear crowded.

On Instagram, you can geotag your photos with the location where they were taken. (with the help of a small technique), and these photos are then put on a Photo Map. When a picture is tagged in this manner, Instagrammers who are nearby or who visit your area at a later time will be able to see your images and interact with them. In turn, this affinity may result in a follow or a visit to your business, and it usually enhances the feeling of location and interest in the photograph. If your company's goal is to reach customers in a certain geographic location, the Places search page may assist you in accomplishing that goal. Related: You may utilize the Top and Most Recent posts from any place to interact with them, and you can use the material you see as inspiration for producing the sort of content popular with people in a given area.

Other people's images are being "programmed." There is no healthier method to attract new consumers to your business than to exhibit photos of existing customers who value what you have to offer. Ask for images to be provided to you by satisfied customers, or - even better - use particular hashtags to search them out on social media. When you discover a photograph you like, use an app like Regram for iOS or PhotoRepost for Android to share it on your social media page. Don't forget to tag the person who originally shot the photo so that they are aware that you used their image. Customers' doodles are often included on the Sharpie website, while Starbucks "piggybacks" on the popularity of Instagram users that have big follow bases by publishing photographs (with permission, of course) that contain their goods.

Chapter Three
Tik-Tok

TikTok has grown worldwide, and many retailers now receive visitors from TikTok. It is not difficult to generate traffic from a platform during its first stages. As a result, it is critical for each seller to have effective TikTok marketing techniques in place to increase their following and traffic.

Conduct Your Research

Without a doubt, studying and getting exceptional information about your area remains critical to success. The first step is to gather as much information as possible about your closest competitors. You must understand the content they produce and deduce the specifics of their success from their videos; this may be challenging, but it is worthwhile to take cautious measures. When you investigate them, you may notice that they make specific errors. You can differentiate yourself by filling a void and doing things differently.

Produce Useful And Creative Content

One of the most enjoyable methods to discover what we like on social media is through videos, which have grown in popularity in recent years. However, to successfully engage our audience and market our business, we must develop valuable and creative videos. In this manner, we can maintain the interest of our fans. Our video appears to be engaging to capture their attention and provide value to our users. Make use of your imagination. Remember that individuals use social media to entertain themselves, so avoid uploading videos that dull the viewer.

Build Partners

If you are committed to operating your business independently, there may be occasions when collaboration with others is unavoidable. If you connect with someone in a similar industry, you can exchange ideas. You could alter one action you have never carried out before and completely transform your traffic. They may also pick up some helpful information from you.

Maintain Consistency

TikTok is the entertainment king, so do everything it takes to assure regular updates and consistency with your TikTok videos, just as you would with a blog.

Increase Your Followers' Engagement. How do you accomplish this? Here are some excellent suggestions:

Submit A Question: It's simple to ask questions about your audience, for instance. How do you feel about the cold weather? This type of inquiry will instill a sense of commitment and affection in them, encouraging them to watch your videos religiously. That is the type of marketing required. Therefore, ask open inquiries frequently.

Invite Your Followers To Vote: Include your audience in the process by presenting them with options; when they reply, you will have already committed them. Allow them to select their position on contentious life problems; this is beneficial because it will stimulate debate. Never take a side with any of your followers. Allow them to discuss matters independently while you serve as moderator.

Make Your Posts During Your Fans' Online Time: Conduct research and determine your fans' internet activity. Thus, by releasing your videos, you will increase your viewership.

Interact With Other Brands: This is highly beneficial since it enables you to market your business to a population that your business never could reach on its own, and a portion of the traffic produced will result in sales. It would be beneficial if you kept in mind that you must share beneficial stuff here.

Crowdsource Comments: You need comments to remain visible to your audience; this is how you'll determine if they enjoy your material or not. One advantage is that individuals have no difficulty validating the comments. It would help if you approached them positively. It would be beneficial if you asked questions to respond to honestly. For instance, where should you focus your next contest's improvements? Will your audience be quick to provide meaningful feedback?

TikTok is very prominent among its end users, yet it can be perplexing and challenging to navigate for people new to it. TikTok is a spin-off of Musical.ly, a platform for social media where users could record themselves lip-syncing to audio snippets, and then the videos are subsequently shared with their pals. To put it simply, It's a video-based app that lets you watch and share videos either by making videos within the application or by posting videos from your mobile. So, why should you be interested in TikTok? How about a billion downloads and installations? That's a significant number of folks who are utilizing the app.

However, aside from its scrolling video feed, there aren't many similarities between TikTok and the Vine app of the same age. TikTok differs from Vine because it is based on concise, six-second films, whereas Vine is more structured. This independence has resulted in various forms and memes that have cropped up on the platform, ranging from quick doodles to DIY photography lessons. As users download the app, more businesses are flocking to it in the hopes of capitalizing on this game-changing platform for marketing purposes. TikTok is primarily a video-based social media site. The app's unique video editing features include filters, music, transitions, unique animations, graphics, and other video editing capabilities. Essential editing functions allow you to tap into your video-making abilities even if you have never used video-editing software before using these functions. Furthermore, similar to other micro-blogging networks, the brief format makes it simple to post and consume the website.

You must be familiar with lingo to comprehend TikTok. To get you started, a few key terms to familiarize yourself with the app are highlighted below:

For You Page: This is the app's home page, where you can find all of its features. For You is a TikTok website that displays a selection of videos that have been hand-picked for you based on your prior viewing history. Following an initial assessment of the types of videos you enjoy, TikTok's algorithm will serve up recommended videos (by grouping together related videos) to each user based on their preferences. Your initial stop on TikTok is the For You page, but like with any platform, if you dig a bit further, you'll discover lively communities based on specific interests.

The Discover Page is where you'll find new content that has been shared on TikTok. The Discover page provides content based on themes, hashtags, viral videos, and other criteria... This is the starting point for exploring the content beyond the For You page.

This is the app section, where you'll find content from the individuals you're following on the platform.

Challenges: The TikTok experience is not complete without the presence of challenges. In this section, creators improve on a video concept created by another user, giving it its own unique touch and flair.

Duets: Duets occur between authors, and you'll find examples of them all around the app, including the home screen. Duets allow other content creatives to work on the contents of other users.

If you're not familiar with the term, a hashtag is a keyword phrase used to classify and aggregate material on social media platforms.

Hashtags are incredibly crucial to TikTok's culture and algorithm, and they are used extensively.

What are the marketing advantages of TikTok?

Using the TikTok application for brand promotion, there are three options available to businesses:

To begin, the user can build their own channel and add videos that they believe are related to their interests.

Second, the user can collaborate with influential individuals to assist their material get shared more broadly over the internet.

Third, the customers can pay for TikTok marketing. However, the platform does not have the same reach as YouTube in terms of audience.

Over time, it may, on the other hand, gain in popularity and stability.

In general, many brands mix their own channels and collaborate with influential persons to reach a broader audience with the content of their products. Furthermore, they can experiment with other concepts on their own channels, such as hashtag challenges, user-generated content, and TikTok advertising.

It is also possible for users to recommend to their influencers that they distribute this type of material in their networks.

Chapter Four

Facebook:

The Ultimate marketing strategy

Facebook is the most popular social network globally, with over a billion users on desktop and mobile. Your target audience will undoubtedly be present because you are the undisputed king of social media. Utilize these techniques to develop, promote, and market your business on Facebook, resulting in an engaged following.

Strategy for Creating a Facebook Business Page Before you plunge in and begin posting on Facebook, It's a smart option to lay some solid foundations for your brand presence so that it's ready to inspire men when they come across your page. Let's start on the road to making your Facebook page a destination worth visiting regularly.

Establish a Facebook Page rather than a personal profile. When you sign up on Facebook, you are automatically assigned a Personal Timeline. Personal Timelines, also known as profiles, are intended for personal, non-commercial usage. While Facebook Pages resemble personal Timelines, they give brands unique resources such as analytics, specific tabs for business-related content, and advertising opportunities. Pages are not required to have a separate Facebook account and do not require a different login from Timelines. A Facebook Page can be created through one of three main ways: by typing 'Create A Page' into the site's search box at the top, by clicking the 'Create A Page' button at the top of any existing Facebook Page, or by clicking the 'Create A Page' button at the top of any current Facebook Page.

If you presently utilize a personal Timeline for business reasons, Facebook may discover and terminate your account without notice. To offer you an opportunity to fix this blunder, Facebook has created a tool that will convert your Timeline to a business Page. When you convert your account to a Facebook Page, your current profile image is maintained, and all of your profile's friends are restored to "like" fans of your Page. Additionally, the username linked with your account will become the identifier of your Page, and the name associated with your account will become the identifier of your Page (you may be able to change this if you wish - I explain how in the next tip). Other content, including wall postings, photographs, and videos, will not be moved over to your new Page, so make sure to download a backup of this data (via your profile settings) if you wish to retain it. If you use your profile for both personal and commercial purposes, the simplest method to avoid getting in trouble is to suspend any business activity on your Timeline, build a separate business page, and then encourage your audience to unfriend your account and "like" your new business account. While a Facebook Page is essential for businesses on Facebook, an individual Timeline offers a variety of non-commercial options to engage with customers and clients on a more personal level.

Maintain a concise Facebook Page name.

Make sure you get it correctly the first time!

If feasible, keep your Facebook Page name short since this will aid in creating Facebook advertising, where the headline space (which is frequently your Page's name) is limited to just 25 characters. You can manually modify the name of a Facebook Page if it has fewer than 200 likes, so choose wisely early on. Navigate to the "About" tab beneath your Page's cover photo if you are dissatisfied with the name of your platform as it is changeable. Save by clicking "Edit" next to the Name section. Changing the name of your Page has no effect on its username or web URL (explained below).

Create a unique web address for your Facebook Page.

For your Facebook Profile, create a temporary URL. (available once you reach 25 likes), preferably one named after your brand; this will make it much easier to direct visitors to your Facebook Page. Consider this carefully since you will only be able to modify this URL once in the future (through the "About" tab); otherwise, you will be forced to erase your Page and start again - not ideal if you have a sizable fan base! To quickly achieve the 25-fan mark, invite your email contacts and current Facebook friends - a group of people who are already invested in you and your brand - to visit and "Like" your Page via the "Promote" drop-down menu at the top of your Facebook Page.

Complete the business information accurately and completely.

Fill in as much information about your company as possible in the About section of your Facebook Page, including the address, contact information, product information, website (use commas to separate multiple URLs in the website box), and links to other social media sites. Customers benefit from your efforts to populate these portions since they consolidate your key information in one place. The keyword-rich blurb is also appropriate for (SEOs), as Google indexes the language in your About section. Are you the restaurant owner, and have you chosen the restaurant/cafe category for your Page? Include the types of items you serve and publish your menu as a PDF for customers to browse; alternatively, if you're in the United States or

Canada, you can add a menu using SinglePlatform. Nota bene: Depending on how your Page is classified, the first-viewed section of the About section may appear differently on the Facebook mobile app than it does on the desktop version. It will display your Short Description to some mobile users, your Mission to others, and a piece of your entire Company Description to yet others. With this in mind, it may be prudent to update each of these elements, beginning with your website URL, to ensure that it is always the first thing mobile consumers see.

Verify your Page and add an official checkmark to your profile picture.

If your business has a physical address in the real world, Facebook allows you to verify your

Page and add an official grey checkmark to its cover photo, similar to the blue checkmark given to celebrities and other famous entities. To authenticate your Page, go to the Page Settings menu and pick Verify Page from the General section. To validate your company representative status, you must contact a publicly listed business phone number or upload an official document, such as a business phone or utility bill, business license, or business tax file. It's well worth the work because Verified Pages rank higher in search results and show users right away that you're the official brand page for your firm on Facebook.

Create an eye-catching cover image and include a call-to-action button.

Because Facebook Page cover photographs can be seen by most people on the platform, it makes the most of the space by successfully communicating your brand or message in a single, high-quality image. The ideal size is 851 315 pixels; any less and Facebook will stretch the image, resulting in a fuzzy appearance. Cover photo ideas include a single strong image that communicates who you are and what you do, a collage of your products, highlighting an ongoing promotion, or featuring a photo or testimonial submitted by one of your fans - the latter will truly "wow" your customer, and hopefully, encourage them to tell their friends. Maintain user engagement by altering your cover photo and profile picture regularly - once a month is an ideal target, but seasonal changes are also popular with firms.

Fundamentals of Facebook Marketing.

Now that your Facebook Page looks beautiful and you're encouraging people to visit it let's look at some strategies to maximize its effectiveness.

Affix significant posts.

For up to a week, You can pin a single post to the top of your Page's Timeline on Facebook. Use this to draw attention to important content and boost the number of people that visit your Page. All new status updates will show beneath the pinned post until it is unpinned (or a week has passed), at which point it will revert to its chronological order. Following creating a post, hover over it until the pencil icon appears, then click it and select 'Pin to Top.' Consider pinning posts that contain special announcements, material, or promotions.

Repost high-quality information, but avoid becoming spammy in your approach.

Given that not everyone checks their Facebook News Feed every day and that only a tiny fraction of your fans will see your material the first time if you have a good article or link to offer, share it multiple times to ensure that as many of your people as possible see it. However, make a concentrated attempt to communicate the information in various ways, for example, by different language in the text, an image with a link, or a link-sharing post. While image-based posts with links are worth experimenting with, standard link-share seats are frequently advised since they mirror how the average user uses Facebook; when was the last time you saw a friend share a link with an uploaded image? Facebook will punish your reach if you frequently publish the same status, as it has discovered that people dislike "copy and paste" updates.

Utilize call-to-actions to increase clicks but prevent "click-baiting."

To increase click-through rates from Facebook and other social media platforms to your website and blog, being precise about what you want your clients to do via a clear call to action is frequently a solid option, e.g., "Click here for additional information [your link]." Frequently, that slight push is all that separates a successful status from one that vanishes without a trace.

Ensure views by utilizing the "Get All Notifications" and "See First" strategies.

One strategy for ensuring that all of your Page's content is seen by all of your fans is to train them to select the "Get Notifications" and "See First" choices located in a drop-down menu when hovering their cursor over the "Liked" and "Following" buttons beneath your Page's cover photo. When this option is selected, whenever you publish a new status update, the fans in question will receive an alert via the blue "globe" icon in their Facebook account's status bar, and your new material will show at the top of that user's News Feed. These requests are best expressed via a status update accompanied by a menu screenshot demonstrating the desired action. It's totally up to you whether you feel at ease asking at the risk of appearing pushy, and your decision should be based on the quality of your relationship with your audience. If you choose to do so, I will not frequently force it on followers, primarily because they are unlikely to be on your Page when your instructions appear and are even less likely to click through and follow-through.

Alternate between videos published on ed on YouTube and those shared on Facebook.

The advent of video content on Facebook has altered the social media environment, and it will continue to do so. Often, it makes sense to upload compelling video content directly to the site instead of sharing a YouTube link; this is because the native Facebook video receives a more equitable distribution of reach (but keep an eye on your analytics to see how things go). If the video is "evergreen" in nature (i.e., It will continue to be as vital in the future as it is now.), why do you need to broadcast it twice - once directly to Facebook and again via a shared YouTube link? Strategies for maximizing the impact of videos submitted to Facebook include having them play automatically – and without audio – within the News Feed. With that in mind, consider how you'll entice fans to watch your clip (and turn on the sound) from the very first frame – catching their eye with movement in the first 2-3 seconds is one way, or if a person is seen speaking in front of the camera, fans who are interested will click to hear what's being said. Using the Video tab on your Page, organize videos into playlists (to encourage increased watch time), and select one video to Feature. The Featured video will feature in a prominent place below the "About" section of your Page's sidebar - a fantastic opportunity to showcase your business or promote a current promotion. Tag individuals who appear in your films, add relevant captions and choose the best thumbnail from the option that displays once the file is posted (or upload your custom image). Additionally, don't forget to download the video embed code in a blog post on your website to increase exposure and interaction — you may opt to embed the full status update or just the video player for a cleaner look.

Solicit Likes and Shares –invite your Page's Likers to do the same.

When you post, encourage users to 'Like' and Share your material so that it is spread on their walls and in their News Feeds, increasing your Page's exposure. Avoid appearing desperate by posting it too frequently (Facebook will limit the reach of these types of posts, especially if the material is terrible), and phrase it in a way that endears you to your fans. Make a direct request, and supporters will pay attention. Enhance the experience by establishing a community that stimulates discussion and interaction among your fans in the comments section.

Additionally, did you know that you can invite folks who have liked a post but not your Page to do so? When a post receives more than a handful of likes, it will display the message "[name], [name], [name], and [number] of others liked this." To view a list of everyone who liked that post and whether they liked your Page or not, click on the "others liked this" link (the chances are that many people will only see your post as a result of someone else engaging with it, and they being notified). If they haven't, you can click "Invite" next to their name to send them an invitation. If they've already loved your content, there's a better likelihood they'll be receptive to seeing it again.

Maintain a timely engagement.

If someone leaves a comment on a status update or a public message on your wall, be careful to respond as quickly as possible. Any opportunity to continue the conversation, respond to a query, or express gratitude for a customer's support is effectively lost without a response - something that many businesses on Facebook fail to do to their harm. If your Page is overflowing and you lack time to respond to each fan comment, giving them a "like" (rather than dismissing them) demonstrates that you are paying attention to what they have to say.

Utilize @mentions to provide a personal touch and increase interaction.

When responding to comments made by specific fans on your Page, utilize the @username method to address each person personally. It will add a personal touch to your service and make the consumer feel unique, all the more so because they will receive notification that you responded. After typing @, immediately begin typing the person's name to whom you wish to reply. When their name appears, click or press it to pick it. If you want to be more informal and address a client solely by their first name, position your cursor at the end of their surname (after it appears in the comment box) and hit backspace several times until their surname vanishes. To that purpose, personalize any status updates or comments you make by 'signing' them with your first name; this is particularly handy if numerous administrators are addressing fans on the same page.

Include timeline milestones and leverage them as marketing opportunities.

By scrolling through and marking dates on your Timeline, Facebook enables you to add Milestones in the history of your business on your Page (e.g., when the business was established, your 1000th sale). These add context to your company's history and provide an intriguing glimpse into your growth over the months and years (mainly if you were in business way before Facebook rolled around). Additionally, you may use future milestones to interact with customers and present them with an incentive to stay connected, for example, "Here's to each of you for contributing to our 20,000-fan milestone! Return tomorrow at 6 p.m. for a special thank-you promotion!". Invite fans to share stories about how your product or service has improved their lives, and then include them - along with accompanying photographs - as milestones demonstrating how invested your consumers are in your business and encouraging others to do the same.

You should thank your newest fans and recognize a fan of the month.

Once a week, send a special 'Thank You're greeting to new fans, including their names if there aren't too many - you can discover them via the "See Likes" option in your Page's Admin Panel; this gives your communication a more personal touch and reflects your brand's image as one that cares about its audience. Launch a "Fan of the Month" initiative to increase your page's engagement. By promoting one of your most devoted fans in this manner, you indirectly inspire other fans to increase their engagement to compete for the coveted title the following month. As an added incentive, provide the winner with a little prize. Several free "Fan of the Month" apps are accessible via the Facebook search bar and commercial ones with additional features.

Chapter Five

The LinkedIn Market: Like a Clockwork, Create a Network

LinkedIn is the web's principal centre for individuals and businesses to connect and advertise their brand, expertise, and abilities to the rest of the world. It was founded in 2003 by Mark Zuckerberg and Reid Hoffman. If you are an individual on LinkedIn, the site can be used to establish a professional profile and control one of the top search results for your name, build a broad network of professional connections whose knowledge you can tap into, and discover new business opportunities, to name a few of the benefits. Creating a LinkedIn business platform allows businesses to communicate more information about themselves, their products and services, job opportunities, and expert insights with their target audiences. Any LinkedIn user can follow a firm that has created a Company Page to receive and interact with updates on their home page, which provides you with an opportunity to raise awareness of yourself and your brand among other LinkedIn users. In a study conducted by LinkedIn, it was discovered that you only need 100-200 followers of your Company Page to reach the tipping point where you can begin making an impact and driving engagement, so it's well worth your time to ensure that both it and your personal profile are performing at their best. Remember, many chapter tips are prefixed with either "Personal Profile" or "Company Pages," Some are prefixed with both. This can help you figure out how to put the advice you've received to good use. Whenever there is no prefix, the tip is a more general hint about one of the many things available on LinkedIn.

Now let us look into some techniques that will help optimize your page both as a personal page or as a Company page profile.

Company/Personal Profile Page Optimization.

LinkedIn Profile (Personal Profile and company profile):

Completely fill out the forms. Fill up all of the parts on your LinkedIn profiles, and make sure you have both a personal LinkedIn page for you as an individual and a LinkedIn Company Page that is mainly for your company - a LinkedIn Business Platform. As a result, you'll want to make a tremendous original outlook for any visitors who land on either of your landing pages.

Sections of your personal Profile that are extremely important:

One of the most significant sections of your personal LinkedIn profile is the Description section since it allows you to go into great detail about your current and previous jobs and responsibilities, as well as your accomplishments. This is a fantastic area to include some relevant keywords, which will increase your chances of ranking higher in LinkedIn's search results. Visitors will know what you've done at each of your positions with a short glance at your personal profile, and they will be able to discover more about you and decide whether you're someone they want to connect with to establish a new professional relationship with you. Short paragraphs or bullet-pointed lists can make a prospect's task even more accessible by making it easy for them to read. If you use bullets, begin your sentences with verbs to make them readable (past tense verbs for past positions, present-tense verbs for present functions). Rather than just pointing out what you did, Rather than just pointing out what you did, describe what you accomplished or how you contributed to the company's success. The more specific and precise you can be in this situation, the better. A vital component of your resume is the summary section, which provides you with your first opportunity to write an overview or statement about yourself and what you can offer your target audience, as well as a chance to demonstrate what makes you exclusive and alluring to potential contacts. Make sure that your Summary accurately reflects your personality. Your company website or LinkedIn Company Page indeed exists to inform people about your company, but your personal profile exists to allow LinkedIn users to discover more about you. Understanding how to create a LinkedIn Business profile is paramount.

Now, to create a LinkedIn Business profile, first, sign in as a personal user and then click on the "Companies" link in the navigation tab near the top of the site's home page.

From here, select the 'Add A Company' button, which is found at the top page on the right-hand side of the page. Before being allowed to begin using LinkedIn, there are a few modest milestones you must achieve and a few easy administrative formalities you must conquer, but you won't be waiting long until you're ready to go! Please keep in mind that to build a LinkedIn

Business profile, you must first have a company email address, such as yourname@yourcompany.com. It is not authorized to use an email address that contains a domain name, such as Outlook or Gmail. You can begin adding info to your Business Page about your region, size, contact information, industry, and other relevant information by choosing Edit in the top-right hand corner of your company's Home tab after it has been created. Sections of the Company Page that are extremely important The 'Company Description' part is, without a doubt, the most crucial. Write a high-level description of your company that highlights your brand and informs readers about what distinguishes you from the competition. It is an excellent area to begin disseminating your message and contacting possible partners and collaborators. It's also a good idea to include a "Specialties" feature on your Business Profile overview. Complete the fields with terms that describe who you are and what you do to increase the likelihood of being discovered more frequently in a LinkedIn search result.

Showcase Pages for specialized items or services:

LinkedIn introduced Showcase Pages in November 2013. It was an interactive replacement for the former "Product and Services" tabs on the company product profile., withdrawn in April 2014. It was a big deal. Showcase Pages and Company Pages are not the same things, and they do not have all of the same features as one another.

Consider Showcase Pages to be the children of the parent website.

Companies can create Company Pages to broaden their LinkedIn presence by posting regular updates about a specific product/service/department/business initiative/etc. Rather than about their entire company as a whole. It also allows them to share unique and distinctive features of their brand with a more focused and targeted audience. Example: Microsoft has a primary Company Page and multiple Showcase Pages for particular products and services on its website. Training and certification in Microsoft Office and other Microsoft products. Showcase Pages can be followed and deliver updates to users the same way they can from any Company Page, so make sure you keep the high-quality content coming with photographs, links, videos, freebies, and other incentives. You should not hesitate to repurpose an update if it appeals to both your more extensive fan base on your principal Company Page and a more niche audience on a Showcase Page. They have their own unique URL for easy sharing, and they also appear on the right-hand side of your Company Page, as shown in the example below. Following the identification of an area (or areas - you can build up to 10 Showcase Pages) of your organization for which a Showcase Page would be beneficial, the following is the procedure for creating a Showcase Page: Instructions on how to establish a Showcase Page are as follows:

1. Click the down arrow next to the coloured Modify button on the Business Page, then select "Create a Showcase Page."

2. Create a new Page and assign administrators to it by entering its name and clicking Create Page.

3. Select Create from the drop-down menu. The following are the optimal Showcase Page branding image sizes: The image for the hero (cover) should essentially be at a minimum of 974 × 330 pixels. The logo is 100 × 60 pixels in size. 50 x 50 pixels for a square logo.

Create a page for your personal profile and carrier for your company:

add a profile photo, a logo, and banner images to your website. Add a recent photo to your personal profile to humanize it - a surprising number of people fail to do so, much to their own cost. The dimensions of LinkedIn profile photos are 200 x 200 pixels. Keep it professional, though: don't put a picture of yourself in your bathing suit on the beach on your LinkedIn page; instead, publish a head and shoulders photo of yourself looking professional and presentable. With your personal information, keep your Profile photo up to date with your changing appearance, including hairstyles, glasses, clothing, and so on. This will ensure that you and your LinkedIn networks are easily identifiable during meetings, conferences, and other events you and your LinkedIn connections attend! In the summer of 2014, LinkedIn began rolling out cover photographs for personal profiles similar to Facebook. According to the guidelines, background photographs should be at least 1400 x 425 pixels in size. Make use of this space to highlight your brand personality, to help people understand who you are, what you do, and how you can assist them - ideas include a photo of yourself, your contact information (email, phone, Twitter handle, etc.), and a call to action (for example, a testimonial). The Home tab serves as the default landing page for your

Business profile on LinkedIn, and it is here that your company logo and banner image will be displayed. However, the size is different from what you see on your Facebook cover image, which is reasonably close. The ideal size for a LinkedIn cover image is 646 222 pixels; the profile photo, which is still square, but has been downsized to 50 x 50 pixels, is the same size as the cover image. Use this space to show and expand on your own branding message. Note: The Premium Content Bundle chapter of this book contains links to download Personal and Company page cover photo templates that are optimized for desktop and mobile displays (as well as a slew of other valuable resources).

Make your personal profile more client-oriented.

LinkedIn users' most common mistake is treating their personal profile as a virtual résumé, not the case. Most potential connections who come across you are not interested in learning about your educational background, your first job, or the accomplishments you have made so far. It is not sufficient to merely introduce yourself to guests. what you do, who you help, how they may help themselves or others in the Summary section at the upper section of your account page. It should also inform what others say about you (short, complimentary quote). Personal profile: think of a clever headline for it. Make your personal LinkedIn profile headline memorable and unique because it is the first piece of information a potential connection will notice about you. "Retail Manager" is a generic title that is not insufficient because millions of those are on LinkedIn. Consider what distinguishes you from others, what makes you unique, and what you want to be recognized for in the world.

Taking a more keen look at Profile Optimization on both personal and company levels, let us understand more steps that could be taken

1. Get a vanity URL for your personal profile. Create your LinkedIn URL of choice when editing your LinkedIn profile by going to the "public profile" area in the editing window. As with other social media platforms, this will make sending potential clients to a memorable address much easier to accomplish.

2. Personal Profile: Make the most of your geographic area. It is possible that entering your location on LinkedIn is not as straightforward as it appears at first glance. If

we consider the case of Merwyn, Illinois, which is a little town just outside of the much larger and better-known metropolis of Chicago - let us pretend for a moment that I am a resident of Merwyn for the purposes of this discussion. The fact that I have listed my location as Chicago will help me appear in more search results (if the search is filtered by location), and I will also be perceived as someone "local" to others in my target market if a prospect scouring LinkedIn was in charge of finding people from the Chicago land area. Consider how this technique might apply to your particular situation and make the necessary changes to your profile.

3. Showcase your accomplishments in your personal profile. Users can add projects,

languages, publications, awards, test scores, courses, patents, certifications, and volunteer work to their LinkedIn profiles. Users can also add photos to their profiles. As you can imagine, If you place yourself in the position of a potential partner, this will significantly enhance your profile in terms of both business and demonstrate your ability to be a well-rounded individual in your field of expertise. So, if you have any other information to share, please do so.

4. Personal Profile: Include rich visual information such as photographs and presentations in your profile. It is feasible to improve the appearance of your LinkedIn profile by including visual content such as images, videos, infographics, and even Slid-

share presentations. This will allow you to highlight your achievements, brands with which you have worked and benefited, your research, and your skills all at the same time. Popular blog entries, screenshots of customer testimonials (such as a tweet or product review), or a video of a fantastic speech you gave at a conference are all examples of unique content to include. Simply click to edit your profile, then click the "+" symbol next to any employment opportunity you're interested in, and then pick whether to upload a file or share a link with other people. It's a no-brainer whenever it concerns Slideshare; you may share an uploaded presentation directly to your LinkedIn profile's Summary section by selecting "Add to profile" from the drop-down menu that displays when you hover

over a presentation in the "My Uploads" part of Slideshare. When you upload new slideshows, the same choice will be available to you.

5. Personal Profile and Company Pages: Use points to make your pages easier to read. If you've completed your LinkedIn profile as its whole, you've likely included a significant amount of information, some of which (achievements, duties, and so on) would be much easier for prospects to read if they were organized in a bulleted list. Although you can use bullet points in your LinkedIn profile sections, this isn't something that the company promotes publicly. Here's how it's done:

- Log into LinkedIn, and from the log option at the top of the screen, pick "Page Edit."

- Navigate to the Profile part where you wish to include bullet points and select the pencil icon.

- "•" should be typed at the beginning of the line to put a bullet point (without the speech marks). You can go through this process as many times as you desire, then click Save.

- You're finished, and your text should be bulleted for easy reading. You might not be allowed to detect the "•" code if you return to edit a section where you have added bullets since it has been replaced with a single space at the beginning of a new line. To get rid of the bullet, delete this space and then hit the Save button.

6. Create your personal profile and company pages with keywords relevant to your company or industry. When you optimize your LinkedIn pages with keywords relevant to you, your expertise, and your business, your pages have a better chance of ranking higher in Google and LinkedIn search results than when they are not optimized. Keep it subtle by not writing in an unnatural style that makes it evident to readers that you are attempting to cram in as many keywords as possible - but be mindful that you'll want to include them regardless of how subtle your writing style is. It's significant to mention in your Profile whenever you gain new skills or knowledge. Fill in as many skills as you can because LinkedIn allows you to add up to 50 skills in total. As a result, you should employ a variety

of keywords ranging from broad ones to those that are more specialized, as you never know what search terms someone else may be used to potentially find you. It is also important where you place these keywords - according to a study conducted by blogging4jobs.com, the terms associated with your name, headline, company name, job title, and talents rank the most. Another crucial area of your personal LinkedIn profile where you should include keywords is the job experience section, including your current and previous roles. Explain your objectives and purpose in considerable detail, going into the same level of detail you would put on your resume. Include any accomplishments and goals that you have met or exceeded. Don't be scared to exaggerate a little!

7. Personal Profile: Rearrange the value of employment roles in your life. By default, LinkedIn will arrange your job positions in chronological order; however, by tapping on the up and down arrow icons beside any position and then picking and releasing it into whatever order you prefer, you can override the system and arrange them according to importance to you (and potential connections).

8. Marketing on LinkedIn and content strategy Personal Profile: Employee profiles can promote your company's image. Getting all of your employees on board with your LinkedIn strategy is critical to its success because it allows you to build a more extensive network

that increases your company's visibility and influence on the social media platform. Instruct your staff to build their LinkedIn profiles and mention your company as their employer on their profiles. As a last resort, provide them with training on creating a great LinkedIn profile. Instead of being concerned that their company's employee profiles will make them a target for headhunters from competing companies, consider them as a reflection of your company's exceptional performance. It is likely that many of your employees already have LinkedIn profiles, and unfortunately, there isn't much you can do to prevent them from leaving if they so choose - the best thing to do is to focus on the positives.

9. Personal Profile: I am a follower of various businesses. Company followers make it easy for you to keep an eye on important events occurring at firms you are interested in, which helps keep tabs on the competition and find inspiration for yourself. From a company's Company Page, you may choose whether or not to follow them. To keep up with a company:

   a. From the log option at the top of your site, select Companies.
   b. Look for a company to work for.
   c. On the company's Home page, click the Follow button in the upper right corner.

   Follow these steps to cease following a company:

- Slide down to the Following section of your Profile after selecting Profile from the log menu at the top of your site.
- To reveal more company details in the Companies section, move your pointer over the preceding grey link below the company's name.
- From the log option, click "Unfollow".

10. Personal Profile: Use Advanced Search and Get Introduced to locate prospects and gain trust, leading to sales or collaboration opportunities. The search and Advanced Search options on LinkedIn are excellent tools for identifying and connecting with possible new prospects. You can narrow down your results by relationships, groups, industry, and region, and you can even store

your search for future reference. Even if you cannot connect with someone directly on LinkedIn, you may be able to gather enough information to contact them outside of the platform, such as through their website or another social profile. Take note that if you click on the "Connect" button next to someone's name in a LinkedIn search, your invitation will be issued automatically, and you will not be given the ability to personalize your message, which is an enormous mistake. Ensure that you click on the person's profile and click the "Connect" button that appears. From here, a box will emerge for you to fill out to create a unique invitation - more information on the best method will be provided shortly. Keep in mind to check the "Persons Who Viewed This Page" box in the righthand sidebar for other people who might make outstanding prospects! Alternative options include utilizing the Get Introduced feature. Contacting members of LinkedIn who are in our 2nd or 3rd-degree network is made possible as a result of this feature. Here's how it's done:

a. Select " Get acquainted through a connection " from the Send, In Mail drop-down menu on the person you wish to connect with, select "Get acquainted through a connection" from the log menu. Should only one of you introduce, the Request an Introduction page will appear. To get introduced, move your mouse pointer over the arrow next to the Send-In Mail button and select Get introduced. If several individuals are capable of making the introduction, you have the option of selecting the person who will make the introduction.

b. Create and send a message to your recipient. When people want to connect with you, be thoughtful and kind in your response. Do the same when you want to connect with others - but avoid being pushy! If you want to customize your invitation, greet them by name and include a brief message that demonstrates that you read and loved a blog post they authored or a lecture they gave in which you were in attendance.

Completing your invitation by providing a compelling cause for you and your guest to engage with one another is recommended. It is possible to make an excellent first impression by including these little extras, which will boost your chances of starting a relationship with someone you are interested in. Once you have established a successful connection with a prospect, write a brief thank-you note and then engage in further conversation to help the relationship grow. Follow-up strategies will change depending on the reasons you linked in the first place and your ultimate goals. Here are some examples: Ideally, you don't want to start pitching your service or product straight away; instead, spend some time getting to know your prospect, possibly by identifying a similarity between you based on the information on their Profile. Simply putting up a reminder utilizing the LinkedIn Contacts tool to "touch base" for several weeks or delivering a free quote, PDF, or another beneficial resource from the goodness of your heart could be enough to make a positive impression. You might consider expanding the conversation to other social media platforms and offline as a method to move things forward toward your end objective, such as offering a product or service or forging a meaningful collaboration, after the relationship has grown sufficiently strong.

11. Personal Profile: Accept invitations that are of high quality and relevance. Along with looking for opportunities to interact with people, you should accept invitations from those who wish to connect with you. The more connections you have, the better. The more comprehensive your expanded network becomes, which in turn opens the door to new opportunities down the road. Unfortunately, spammers can be found on LinkedIn, as they can be found on many

social media platforms, so be cautious to only accept invitations from credible and appropriate profiles.

12. Utilize tags and notes to neatly manage your connections on your personal profile page. The Contacts function on LinkedIn (which can be reached via the Networks option) displays a list of all of your relationships on the social networking site. Tagging individuals with specific characteristics with unique labels is one of its uses. By doing so, You'll have the opportunity to categorize and organize different types of individuals (such as hot prospects, existing clients, thought leaders, and so on) to sort, find, and contact them as quickly and efficiently as possible whenever the need arises. Simply click on the tag icon to

the right of a contact's name, select from the suggested tags list, or create your own. After that, you may use the Tags option to filter connections based on their tags. When you click on a contact's complete Profile, you will see a "Relationship" option, denoted by a star. This is an additional step in improving organization and efficiency. There are various options available when you click this, including an area to make comments about that person, a place to add how you met, and a function to create reminders about them, such as when you need to follow up with them. Each piece of information in this part is only accessible by you. Please keep in mind that your Contacts page will also notify you of critical developments in the professional lives of your connections, such as when they begin a new position. Remember to send a brief letter to express your appreciation for a contact's accomplishment, stay in touch, and continue strengthening your relationship.

Chapter Six

Pinterest as a Media Platform

Pinterest permits anyone to fashion and establish virtual pinboards on virtually any theme, and then stake these pins (which are most frequently images but can also be in video form) with other Pinterest operators as well as with individuals all over the globe via websites, blogs, and other social networks. Alternatively, pins can be posted directly from your computer or mobile device, or they can be shared through a website. Pinterest's popularity has skyrocketed since the site's introduction in March of 2010. As a result, when you consider that Pinterest is the second most important driver of web traffic among social media sites (behind only Facebook), it should come as no surprise that tens of thousands of businesses, including the world's largest, are already utilizing the site to showcase their brand to an audience of over 70 million users, with more than 75 per cent of those users accessing the site via mobile devices. Pinterest users come to the site to search for, browse, and collect the things that fascinate and inspire them - and it is here that the enormous potential for companies on the site comes into play, as many of them are shoppers. Individual or business, the most successful Pinterest pins all have a few things in common: they combine eye-catching photos with information that solves a problem, inspires a user, offers something valuable, or appeals to a user's interest in a certain hobby or activity. Contemplate how these pinnable characteristics can be applied to your brand as a way for people to discover content about the things they love that you have previously pinned - to encourage engagement and conversation about your company culture, products, and services, and to drive click-through rates to your content that isn't hosted on the Pinterest platform. If a vendor of bespoke dog collars publishes pins on how to teach dogs tricks or how to make homemade dog treats, this is an example of affiliate marketing. While some Pinterest users come to the site with the express intent of finding a product to purchase, others do not or are at a different stage of the purchasing process.

***

As a result, the combination of content you supply should be appealing to and beneficial to both types. To summarize: If the content you post inspires someone to purchase from you, that's fantastic (Pinterest users frequently create "wish list boards" as a stepping stone to purchasing products, so you'll want to encourage them to add your products to these while browsing), but if it makes them laugh, smile, daydream, or think positively about you, that's also fantastic. Pins that are not just promotional in nature but also lifestyle-based and influential due to their good association with your company can be just as useful in the long term as promotional pins. Whether your material provides a useful suggestion or inspires a user to take action, it will only increase the likelihood that they will repin it to one of their boards for safekeeping and display it to their followers via their Home screens, as described above. If you have a passion for inspiring people with words and photos, you should use Pinterest, no matter what type of business you have. Demonstrate their objectives and dreams to them. This means that you should create boards that highlight your products and services and boards that demonstrate fascinating and pinnable ideas, topics, and concepts related to your products and services. Although your company might not be particularly very visually oriented and you, on the other hand, might not believe Pinterest would be a good fit for your needs, it's important to realize that the site is as much (if not more) about collecting and sharing photos created by others as it is about pinning your own. For example, a coffee shop might include a board with information on their drinks and food and the newest trends in coffee culture - gadgets, music, interior design, and so on - on which customers can comment. People re-pin and follow accounts on Pinterest because they are relevant to their interests and needs, not because they are enthusiastic about your latest marketing effort! Be a resource for pinners and approach your pins with a service mindset rather than a profit-driven one. Optimization of your Pinterest profile Although Pinterest's present structure does not provide a great deal of flexibility for altering the appearance of your profile, there are still a few important things you should consider doing to maximize the impact of your account... Become a registered business (or adapt your private Pinterest profile account) Since its launch in November 2012, Pinterest has increased its support for brands, including the ability for them to register specifically as businesses (rather than just as individuals), putting into consideration also, the ability for those brands that already had a Pinterest presence to convert their personal accounts to business accounts. To do either, go to http://business.pinterest.com and select the one that pertains to you from the drop-down menu.

***

Once you've registered as a business on Pinterest, you'll have access to a variety of business-specific resources, such as Pinterest analytics tools, successful case studies, and links to Pinterest buttons and widgets that you can use to advertise your activity on the site on your website or blog. Make a memorable username for yourself. When creating a Pinterest account, the first thing you'll want to make sure you get right is your username, which will serve as the basis for your Pinterest profile's URL. You will want to market this URL online and in-person, making it as short, straightforward, and memorable as possible. Although your brand image is the most logical alternative, examine whether or not you have a keyword or slogan associated with it that would work better (especially if your brand's name is larger than the 15-character restriction). Furthermore, your 'First Name' and 'Last Name' must reflect your brand because they will be shown prevalently somewhere at the top of your Pinterest account. For example, I may go by the identities 'The Social media market strategist' and 'Marketing Tips, as my first and last names. Although, if your organization's name is short, it may not be required to include the last name. Make use of the information in the 'About' section. If you create a detailed description in the About area of Pinterest, it will be located precisely at the top-right of your profile page and serves to describe your brand and what you do. Aside from showing up more frequently in your search result, you must include two or three of your company's most important keywords in the description under your Pinterest URL. Don't go overboard with the character count - 160 characters should be sufficient. Add your website and check it for trustworthiness before submitting it. This one is very self-explanatory. When someone visits your profile, a small 'globe' icon will be displayed at the very top of the page, which, when clicked, will take them to your website. It isn't prominently displayed on the Pinterest profile page, but every little bit helps, so don't forget to fill it out. You can authenticate your website on Pinterest to show others that you are a trustworthy source of information. Once you've validated your account in your profile, you'll see a checkmark next to the URL. As well as access to Pinterest site analytics. To have your website verified on Pinterest, simply click the "Verify Website" button that appears next to the field where you typed your website's URL. Follow the on-screen directions to finish the verification procedure on the following page. Verification can be accomplished by using an HTML file or a meta tag. Create an eye-catching profile picture. Your company's insignia and, if you're the company's figurehead, a head and shoulders shot of yourself are the two most prevalent types of Pinterest profile photographs for brands - of course, smiling and looking pleased. Pinterest profile photographs are displayed within a rounded square on your profile page, as well as within circles adjacent to pinned content and comments, and within circles next to pinned comments. Ensure that your brand is visible in the centre of the 200 by 200-pixel image and keep your company logo or face within the middle "safe region," away from the corners, to guarantee that it looks excellent anywhere it appears on the site. Download a prototype to help you do so (as well as a slew of other useful resources) from the Premium Content Bundle chapter of this book. Strategy for using Pinterest as a marketing and content distribution channel Following the completion of your Pinterest profile page, let's look at the marketing and content tactics that will assist you in taking advantage of every possibility that the platform has to offer. Optimum The dimensions and design of Pinterest pin images Pinterest does not impose any restrictions on the vertical dimension of photographs pinned to its boards, but the horizontal width of images is limited to 735 pixels at the most. Any image width is acceptable; however, It would be adjusted to a maximum resolution of 735 pixels and shown as such. Also, keep to heart the following: Pinterest only allows users to pin from web pages that have at least one image, and these photos must be a minimum dimension of 110 x 110 pixels to be permitted to pin. To encourage others to pin from your website or blog, include at minimum one pinnable image on every page or article. The use of taller photos on Pinterest, according to research, results in more re-pins because they work better with the way the site stacks different pieces of material on top of each other in its infinitely-scrolling, narrowly barred grid. As a result, if you want your photographs on your Pinterest account and blog to be shared more frequently on Pinterest, make them as tall as possible. Naturally, this isn't always practical, but there are several simple methods to include this strategy into your Pinterest activity using picture kinds like infographics and step-by-step "how-to" posts (both of which are detailed below). When it comes to colour and design, a year-long study by Curalate, a Philadelphia-based startup, found that images (particularly of products) taken against a plain and minimalist background performed better on Pinterest (in contrast to most other social networks) than those with too much in the frame (in contrast to most other social networks). Additionally, photos that are too light or too dark were shown to perform poorly - images in the centre of the spectrum performed best. Pins that had numerous dominating colours (rather than just one) were observed to garner greater attention, while bright and warm colours such as orange and red were observed to be re-pinned more frequently than "colder" colours such as blue were observed to receive less attention. And last but not least, it discovered that photographs without human faces performed best on Pinterest - arguing that this is because the site is a social media platform of "things," where faces are merely a distraction, as opposed to sites such as Facebook, which is a type of social media interconnection of people. I propose that you take these trends with a grain of salt and keep a careful eye on which material works best for you and your target audience as you create your Pinterest strategy. When and what to pin - Maintain a consistent and innovative approach. Pin on a steady and regular basis - a few times a day is a good goal - but keep the stream moving steadily, rather than letting it go for weeks with no activity followed by a flurry of activity. This method will increase your exposure and prevent your followers from being inundated with messages. If you want to increase the exposure of your Pinterest content, don't be afraid to pin it more than once. Don't pin it to the same board repeatedly (choose one with a similar fit or a group board), and don't pin it immediately after the initial share - always give the original pin time to shine before pinning again. What you publish will be determined by your business or company, but given that studies show that approximately 80% of Pinterest's content comprises re-pinned pins, make an effort to generate original and exciting pins to guarantee that you are included in the magical other 20% of the content. Using the following method when posting a pin that involves a product may be beneficial: one photo of the product on its own (for example, with a simple white background) and another photo of the product in the environment where it will be utilized (e.g., luxury towels in a bathroom). The former technique allows followers to picture how the product can fit into their lives, while the latter allows them to pin basic photos for inspiration. Remember to link both pins to the same sales page on your website, as well as the other way around. When you share information from others, you can establish yourself as an authority in your field by sharing motivational content. Engaging, accurate, up-to-date, helpful, and insightful content. In addition to being an advertisement for your brand, other Pinterest users' boards tell a great deal about their likes, interests, hopes, and aspirations. Make the most of this knowledge to transform your profile into a destination that benefits your audience. Select "Popular" from the drop-down menu on the Pinterest home page to learn more about what's popular with Pinterest users right now, and then determine whether it is appropriate for you to incorporate these trends into your content strategy: Share pins from other boards that your followers will love to make your profile a more valuable asset. Note: Pinterest uses a "smart feed" algorithm to determine the distinction of a pin is built on the beauty of the image it contains and the management structure of the website from which it was pinned - The quality of a pin is determined by the number of people that pin it on the site. Pins that combine these two characteristics are preferred in the site's feed because they are more visually appealing. It's hard to know whether or not your pins are being singled out for special treatment by the smart feed algorithm, but being aware of this back-end procedure should motivate you to regularly share only the greatest content. Keep the names of your boards short and simple. Even while you should use keyword-rich titles for your boards, you should make the names basic and descriptive so they can be found readily in Pinterest's search - yet short enough so that the names do not trail off when viewed on your profile. When viewed on your profile page, each of your board names can have up to 30 or so characters (including spaces) before being cut off - the remaining characters can be seen when the board is clicked on. In contrast, the cut-off point for Pinterest searches is significantly shorter, at roughly 20 characters. If the name of your message board is more than 20 characters, attempt to include the most relevant keywords at the beginning of the name to increase the likelihood that other users will notice it. It's critical to select your Pinterest account theme precisely because it will become part of its URL, i.e., www.pinterest.com/your-board-name (important for SEO). Note: Because several individuals use Pinterest as a search engine (in some cases, preferring it over Google for specific searches), approaching the setup of your content on the site with an SEO mindset is important - in board names, pin names and descriptions, and even the file name of your images - is important (more on these shortly). Keep the term "niche" in mind when establishing boards. While browsing Pinterest, you may have noticed that some of the most well-known brands have built a large number of pinboards, each of which contains content that is highly relevant to the brand's identity. However, while overloading your profile with pins may seem counter-intuitive to the "less is more" school of thought, it may actually prove beneficial in the long run. Why? Because several individuals use Pinterest search to find content (or come across it via a web search), having highly targeted boards increases the likelihood that your pins will be discovered and viewed. Consider the following example: a board titled "Wedding Inspiration" is highly general - there are thousands of other boards with the same name, and the chances of yours getting discovered if you are just starting out as a wedding accessories dealer are poor. Although less likely to be looked for, a board called "Pink Wedding Dresses 2014" has significantly less competition, giving it a greater chance of being discovered in search results than a board called "White Wedding Dresses 2014." So, while creating your Pinterest boards, think about what makes them distinct, particular, and niche, and target the material and phrases you believe your target audience will be looking for. Choose a visually appealing board cover. As a board cover, one pin from each of your Pinterest boards will be selected from your collection of pins. Your profile picture and search results should have eye-catching, beautiful, and accurately represent the board as a whole. In a nutshell, your board cover should entice people enough to make them want to click on it and read the entire material. To choose a pin as the cover for a board on your profile, hover over the board in question and click the 'Change Cover' button on your keyboard. Use the arrows to navigate to the pin you want to use as the cover for your board. When choosing your board cover image, you have the option of repositioning the image so that the best section of the image is seen on the cover. To make the modification effective, click Save Changes. Reorganize your Pinterest boards according to their value. Pinterest gives you the ability to reorganize the boards on your profile page. It's as simple as clicking, holding, and dragging boards into their optimal placements from your profile page. The aim here is to move your most significant boards to the first few rows - particularly those that are 'above the fold,' that is, visible onscreen before a user has to scroll down to access more boards. Consider which of your boards you want to highlight the most prominently - whether it's based on seasonal promotions, holidays, current trends, or anything else - and place them in the most important real estate regions of your Pinterest profile, such as the header and footer. Create secret boards to collect pins and strategize marketing campaigns. Create an unlimited number of secret boards that can be made public at any moment in the future with

Pinterest's 'Secret Boards' function. One simple and effective application of Secret Boards is seasonal marketing, such as Valentine's Day, Thanksgiving, Christmas, and other holidays. As you slowly accumulate content for your campaign's themed Secret Board throughout the year, you'll be well prepared to make it public when the time comes. You'll have a ton of material to choose from, and then you can continue to add to it during the campaign's promotional period. To create a Secret Board, choose the option located at the extreme lower part of your homepage; or, when creating a board from the 'Add' menu, be sure to toggle the Secret Board slider to the 'On' position as described above. Effective pin descriptions will increase re-pins and web traffic. Pinterest is one of the most important website traffic sources globally; creating excellent pin descriptions is critical to providing your content with the best possible chance of getting discovered when a user searches the site. Since the launch of Pinterest's Guided Search in April 2014, optimizing your pin descriptions has become even more important (a feature that provides fast keyword ideas and inspiration to assist users in discovering exactly what they are looking for). The primary recommendation is to come up with the best pin captions in the manner of a useful and searchable piece of information, including specific and distinct keywords that reflect the pin's content and your business, for example, "red, V-neck striped red sweater from Karen's Apparel, Denver" is much more effective than simply "wool sweater." As a rule, if the pin requires it, descriptions that explain how the subject of the pin adds value function better than direct explanations, so think about what a potential buyer might want to know and write with that in mind. Instead of saying something like "We're now selling these diamond earrings, let us know what you think of them," a more effective description might read something like, "The way that the light bounces off these beautiful diamond earrings is mesmerizing, and they'd look great with just about any outfit for a night out on the town. " In your pin description, provide a call to action. According to some studies, it can help increase the number of clicks on your pin, so you may want to include one in your description.

Conclusion

In modern days, the things you can accomplish with social media are almost endless, and that limitation can only exist in your imagination. To sum up, you will agree with me that we are better off now than we were ten years ago in terms of marketing and placing items into a wider viewing range. The Internet has already changed people's lives, and social media has contributed to that optimism by making selling and buying faster and more efficient, making product providers' and sellers' jobs easier. This will work for those prepared to put in the effort, and it will be a massive money-making operation.

Printed in Great Britain
by Amazon